Bill Russell in Chicago, January 1956. Photograph by Natty Dominique

JAZZ
Scrapbook

**BILL RUSSELL and
SOME HIGHLY MUSICAL FRIENDS**

THE HISTORIC NEW ORLEANS COLLECTION
1998

Cover and title-page illustration: Michael Ledet
Essay illustrations: adaptations of Bill Russell's American Music record labels
All other illustrations in this volume from the William Russell Jazz Collection,
The Historic New Orleans Collection, unless otherwise noted

Library of Congress Cataloging-in-Publication Data

Jazz scrapbook : Bill Russell and some highly musical friends.
    p.   cm.
   Includes bibliographical references.
    Contents: Bill Russell / Jon Kukla — Jelly Roll Morton / Mark Cave —
Louis Armstrong / Carol Bartels — Bunk Johnson / M. Theresa LeFevre —
Mahalia Jackson / Nancy Ruck — Baby Dodds / Dan Ross — Natty
Dominique / John Magill — Fess Manetta / Richard Jackson — The
Russell Collection / Alfred E. Lemmon.
    ISBN 0-917860-41-1 (pbk. : alk. paper)
    1. Jazz musicians—United States—Biography. 2. Sound recording
executives and producers — United States — Biography. 3. Russell,
Bill, 1905-1992. 4. Russell, Bill, 1905-1992 — Archives. I. Historic
New Orleans Collection.
ML394.J42   1998
781.65'092'2—dc21

                                      98-14760
                                          CIP
                                         MN

CONTENTS

Charles Edward Smith, Bill Russell, and Frederic Ramsey, Jr., July 1941.
Smith and Ramsey edited the classic *Jazzmen* in which Russell's essays appeared.

Bill Russell. Photograph by Frank Krencik

LP
33⅓

GOOD
STRING

AMERICAN MUSIC
NEW ORLEANS

BILL RUSSELL

Bill Russell [William Russell; born Russell William Wagner] (1905-1992) studied the violin, but by the early 1930s emerged as a composer of avant-garde music for percussion instruments. His fascination with jazz, however, soon came to overshadow his own musical career. He rediscovered Bunk Johnson, undertook a historic series of recordings of older jazz musicians such as Baby Dodds, Bunk Johnson, Dink Johnson, George Lewis, Wooden Joe Nicholas, and Jim Robinson, and became a confidant to Mahalia Jackson. He devoted his life to collecting material on jazz and its origins, completing a book on Jelly Roll Morton shortly before his death.

Bill Russell. Photograph by Gary Vitrano. Courtesy Peggy Scott Laborde, WYES-TV

BILL RUSSELL

When Bill Russell died on August 9, 1992, the shelves and boxes that held his immense jazz collection filled the ground floor of his Orleans Street house. Treasures were everywhere: vintage records and photographs, reel-to-reel tapes, jazz periodicals and sheet music, correspondence and notes, his record player, and some musical instruments. Silhouetted against a window, on a desk-high shelf just inside the back room, half a dozen recent incoming letters lay face down in a shallow cardboard box, ready for Russell to jot notes or a reply on the backs. The same shelf held two more boxes, now empty, labeled "String" and "Good String." Call it the collector's impulse or call it frugality. Both were correct. In life and music, Bill Russell knew the good string.

As the world learned of his death, the *Times* of London summarized his profound gifts to the cultural history of the twentieth century in a simple declarative sentence: "Bill Russell was the single most influential figure in the revival of New Orleans jazz that began in the 1940s." Russell, the obituary continued, had kindled interest in the subject in his thought-provoking contributions to the 1939 book *Jazzmen*. He furthered it by helping to rediscover and later record the pioneer trumpeter Bunk Johnson, and he consolidated it through the series of recordings of other pioneers he made for his American Music record label from 1944 to 1955.

Even this glowing tribute, from a newspaper inclined more to understatement than exaggeration, omitted important dimensions of William Russell's life and career. Violinist, composer, teacher, archivist, record producer, historian, and humanist — Russell merged his vast knowledge of music and his passion for its transforming role in the lives of individuals and societies into a sixty-year quest to preserve and appreciate American jazz and its place in world history.

Although he carefully registered copyrights for his writings and musical compositions in the name of William Russell, marked items in his jazz collection with the letters *WR*, and answered to thousands of jazz enthusiasts as Bill Russell, he was born in Canton, Missouri, on February 26, 1905, as Russell William Wagner. From his first-generation German-American parents he inherited a love of music and aspirations for perfection — influences that later prompted his altered name (for the world already had one great Wagner). Early in life he was attracted to drums, but his mother's encouragement of the violin led eventually to a diploma in violin, music history, and music theory from the Quincy Conservatory of Music. A youthful orchestral arrangement based on a classical sonata won fourth prize in a *Chicago Daily News* contest, and at Culver-Stockton College,

Bill Russell in the late 1920s. Original photograph owned by William Wagner

Russell played violin in the orchestra. Later, he studied with Arnold Schoenberg in California; Ludwig Becker, concertmaster of the Chicago Symphony; and Max Pilzer, concertmaster of the New York Philharmonic.

At the Teachers College of Columbia University he was captivated by African and Asian music. The latter interest blossomed as he traveled throughout the United States from 1934 to 1939 as musician and arranger with the Red Gate Shadow Players. Russell kept a scrapbook of the group's performances (including one in the Roosevelt White House): announcements, clippings, letters, photographs, and programs, all in careful sequence. Between these tours of the 1930s, Russell emerged as a collector, composer, and fan of jazz.

Virtually unknown to the general public, Russell's compositions for percussion ensemble are pivotal works in the modern classical music tradition. In 1931, his *Fugue* was premiered in the same concert with Edgar Varèse's *Ionization*. Six decades later, experimental composer John Cage arranged a New York concert of Russell's entire oeuvre that was issued on compact disc as *Made in America: The Music of William Russell*. Russell was among the radical musicians of the 1930s, schooled in the classical tradition, who fomented a revolution of musical aesthetics. His avant-garde percussion compositions, like the music of Cage and Varèse, pulled threads from the fabric of European music, but Russell also wove jazz themes into his works. His music reflected a conviction that truly independent

American art draws upon all the nation's ethnic traditions. Good string, indeed.

By chance, or destiny, during these same years Russell began collecting jazz recordings. While teaching at a small school in New York City in 1929, he found a discarded recording of Jelly Roll Morton and His Red Hot Peppers playing "Shoe Shiner's Drag." Russell took the record home, listened to it, and never got over it. Jazz was exciting. He opened the Hot Record Exchange in 1935 with painter Steven Smith, reselling records he had gathered. He began writing for *Jazz Hot*. On February 26, 1937, William Russell made his first pilgrimage to New Orleans (which he visited again each year until he moved there for good in 1956). In 1939, Russell's reputation as a jazz authority was secured with the publication of his world-renowned selections in *Jazzmen*, a pioneering work edited by Frederic Ramsey, Jr., and Charles Edward Smith. The research for that book led to his rediscovery of trumpeter Bunk Johnson, whose recordings and touring performances brought New Orleans jazz to a new generation of listeners.

The work with Bunk Johnson, in turn, led Russell to found his American Music record label. Despite his extensive musical education and promising career as a serious composer, he now devoted his energies to recording "the best music I had ever heard." Academicians may argue about who invented jazz. The question did not trouble Russell, but documenting the African American musical heritage became more

Bill Russell at the Caldonia Club, St. Claude and St. Philip Streets, New Orleans

Bill Russell with tuba, 1958

important to him than composing. To capture the sound of this American music, Russell lugged his cumbersome recording machine and heavy boxes of glass-based acetates from San Francisco to New Orleans to Chicago. The 78s that he produced were well cut and clearly labeled. The LPs were even better. His liner notes are small gems of jazz literature. Eventually his recordings would be reissued in Denmark and Japan, and in 1987 he sold his American Music label to the GHB Jazz Foundation, which continues to reissue many of Russell's recordings as compact discs.

In the 1950s, Bill Russell helped to establish the Archive of New Orleans Jazz (now Hogan Jazz Archive) at Tulane University, which awarded him an honorary doctorate. The International Percussive Arts Society also honored him for his role in the development of twentieth-century percussion music, and the International Association of Jazz Record Collectors, for his contributions to the world of recorded jazz, but Russell cared little about these accolades. The music and its cultural context were what mattered. Gathered in his French Quarter home were more than 36,000 artifacts — books, recordings, letters, news clippings, periodicals, photographs, postcards, sheet music, and taped interviews — that testify to his erudition and dedication. For those who might not hear it in the music itself, here was proof of his vision that jazz had developed not in a vacuum but within a complex New Orleans environment shaped by myriad influences. All kinds of string.

Bill Russell sorting records

Russell became a resource, influence, mentor, and friend to aspiring performers and scholars of jazz worldwide. Many of his friends people this book. Night after night he sat at the door of Preservation Hall, the mecca of revitalized jazz tradition, selling records and tapes to tourists waiting to hear the jazz masters he championed. Few of those tourists standing in line along St. Peter Street knew that the man in a plaid shirt selling them records was himself a celebrated contributor to American culture.

In September 1992, a month after Bill Russell's death at eighty-seven, the Historic New Orleans Collection became the permanent home of his entire jazz archive. This final development was very much Bill Russell's idea, another testimony to the profound convictions that shaped his life and career. "If a person really has the right kind of music in their mind, heart & body," Russell wrote in 1951, "they are likely to think and act right, . . . be happy, love everyone and hate no one. . . . If all this sounds like a religion I'm sorry, but until these ideas can be proven wrong I'll go on believing."

Bill Russell's generous American spirit continues to inspire those who work with the William Russell Jazz Collection. He <u>was</u> "the single most influential figure in the revival of New Orleans jazz" because it was the best music he had ever heard. He knew good string.

—Jon Kukla

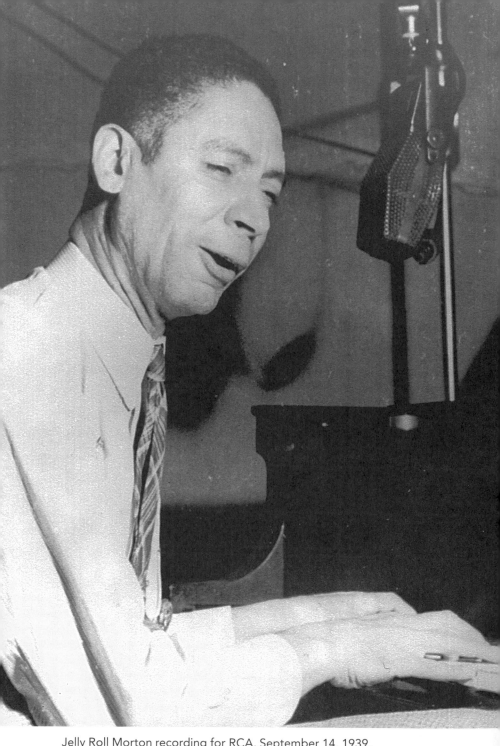

Jelly Roll Morton recording for RCA, September 14, 1939.
Photograph by Otto Hess?

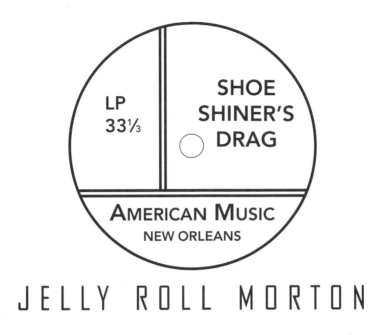

LP
33⅓

SHOE
SHINER'S
DRAG

AMERICAN MUSIC
NEW ORLEANS

JELLY ROLL MORTON

Jelly Roll Morton (1890-1941) is considered by many to be the first important jazz composer, the one who polished the New Orleans style to perfection. This self-styled inventor of jazz was a native of New Orleans whose birth date and name have been matters of dispute. He was baptized Ferdinand Joseph Lemott (also rendered La Menthe or La Mothe); he adopted Morton as his stage name, an anglicized version of Mouton, his stepfather's name. Learning to play the piano early, he began his musical career playing in the bordellos of Storyville. He achieved great success with his Red Hot Peppers in Chicago during the 1920s, helping to popularize the New Orleans style. Some of his more notable compositions include "Grandpa's Spells," "Black Bottom Stomp," and "The Pearls."

Jelly Roll Morton in New York, 1930s. Photograph attributed to Danny Barker

JELLY ROLL MORTON

In 1929, while teaching music in New York City, Bill Russell happened on some jazz records left behind by a student. The quirky title "Shoe Shiner's Drag" caught his eye: the tune would spark a lifelong devotion to jazz music and its self-anointed founding father, Jelly Roll Morton. Nine years later, after amassing a nearly complete collection of Jelly Roll's recordings, Russell sought Morton out in Washington, D.C. Morton had fallen on hard times by 1938, supporting himself as a manager, piano player, and waiter at a floundering club called the Music Box.

Russell recalled their meeting with precision: "The room was fairly large, but rather narrow, about 20 by 35 feet, and took up the entire second floor except for the stairway, the hall and the kitchen." He was surprised that Morton was so accommodating to an unknown fan. They talked for awhile and played some recordings on the juke box. Jelly Roll later sat at the piano and played "King Porter Stomp," "The Pearls," and "Wolverine Blues." He apologized for his playing, complaining that his fingers were stiff, but Russell thought it was terrific.

Russell was in Washington with the Red Gate Shadow

Players and managed several trips to the Music Box to talk to Jelly Roll. Morton had gathered around him a small group of jazz devotees which included writer Charles Edward Smith, collector Roy Carew, and folklorist Alan Lomax, then interviewing Morton for the Library of Congress. Russell joined the select group talking about the origins of jazz with Morton and listening to him play. On one occasion Russell was late to work because of a gathering at the Music Box, which he later recalled as an indication of his priorities. At their last encounter in Washington, Morton told Russell of his intended return to the top: "The king is coming back."

They met again on September 21, 1940, at the Rhythm Club in New York, where Jelly vented his frustrations with music publishers and musicians, claiming that he had not been given proper credit for his work and as a result had been cheated out of a million dollars. He told Russell about his plans for his new "big band" and invited him to come to rehearsals. Russell did not attend: looking back, he was to remark that his absence was an "embarrassing indication of my stupidity." Jelly Roll died less than a year later in Los Angeles.

Perhaps it was regret over this missed opportunity that moved Russell to devote so much time to uncovering the true story of Jelly Roll's life — a task not easily accomplished. As basic a fact as Morton's birth date was hard to establish. The preferred date among jazz researchers is October 20, 1890, based on a baptismal certificate for Ferdinand Joseph Lemott.

Jelly Roll Morton, probably before 1920. Photograph from the Al Rose Collection, courtesy William Ransom Hogan Jazz Archive, Tulane University

Jelly Roll himself gave different dates—1885 and 1897. Published sources have listed his year of birth as 1886 and 1889. And to further complicate matters, the 1900 U.S. census indicates that he was born in 1894. Russell, perhaps out of respect for Morton, did not stand wholeheartedly behind any date. He remarked, "So what difference does it make when he was born? If we make Jelly a few more years younger he'll be in a class with the child prodigy Mozart."

Russell interviewed many of the musicians who played with Morton, as well as his surviving friends and family members. Any interview is, of course, slanted by the perspectives of both interviewer and subject, but the sheer bulk of Russell's work permits the researcher to confirm details again and again. As a result, a fairly reliable account of Jelly Roll emerges.

Style always mattered to Morton. "In New Orleans," Kid Ory remembered, "Jelly Roll wore striped colored silk shirts, and he used garters to hold up his sleeves. One time he had a high roller hat, turned up. It was a soft hat with a wide brim. I told him, 'you look like a cowboy.'" Morton's younger sister Frances Oliver described him in Chicago in 1925: "His hair was very long. He used to comb it from the front all the way back. He was so particular about his teeth, he had two or three of them capped. The diamond showed up all the time. It was in an upper tooth right next to his right eye tooth."

According to Danny Barker, Jelly Roll was "his own press agent." His inclination for self-promotion rubbed a lot of

Site of the Music Box, 1211 U Street, Washington, D.C., where Jelly Roll Morton worked in 1938. Photograph by Bill Russell taken in 1968

Jelly Roll Morton's Red Hot Peppers, ca. 1926. Left to right, Andrew Hilaire, Kid Ory, George Mitchell, John Lindsay, Jelly Roll Morton, Johnny St. Cyr, and Omer Simeon

people the wrong way. Those who knew him well, however, viewed his pretensions as comedy, an expression of poor self-esteem, or a business ploy. About 1940, his business cards read "World's Greatest Hot Tune Writer." A boastful style was not uncommon among traveling musicians of that era — a good way of attracting attention in a new town and landing jobs. It seems to have worked for Morton. Johnny St. Cyr remarked that Jelly Roll would "talk himself into the best jobs in the country."

It was in the sporting houses of Storyville that Jelly Roll's musical talents were nurtured. Kid Ory recalled: "They called him Windin' Boy because he used to wind when he walked, you know. The women liked that, so he'd walk that way, his hat to one side, and one suspender down." Fess Manetta remembered that Jelly Roll had "a funny disposition, funny ways. He fooled around and gambled at the 25s [Club], played cotch." Despite his "funny ways," he was one of Storyville's best performers.

Jelly Roll thrived on performance. He believed that the only true music was that played directly to an audience. He did make records, which were quite successful in the twenties, but felt that recording was just a way to get a little money and promote his name. His love of live performance kept him on the move most of his life — from the Gulf Coast to St. Louis, Memphis, California, Chicago, New York, Washington, Mexico, Canada, and countless places in between. Morton's wanderlust presents a challenge for his biographers.

In the late sixties Russell began work on a Morton biography, a book he modestly said "Roy Carew should have written." Carew had also met Jelly Roll at the Music Box in Washington. They became such good friends that they established the Tempo Music Publishing Company together to publish Jelly Roll's arrangements and secure copyrights. As an employee of the Internal Revenue Service, Carew had the financial and legal skills Morton lacked.

When Morton loaded his worldly possessions into his Cadillac on Christmas Eve 1938 and left Washington for New York, his relationship with Carew continued. Their letters, although primarily about business, reveal a deepening friendship and genuine concern for each other's welfare. They document the last few years of Jelly Roll's life, saddened by professional frustrations and failing health. Morton's letter of March 19, 1938, is typical: "Just two days ago I would have much rather been dead than alive, with so many different pains, I felt, that I've been worried on a very large scale, simply because I haven't been able to do the things I want."

Roy Carew was protective of the memory of his friend. In a letter to Bill Russell dated March 5, 1944, he wrote, "I would want any Notes to a folio or book of Jelly's music to be written by someone who has a real regard for him, and for his music." Carew had long intended to put together a book about Jelly Roll. As early as 1950 Alan Lomax inscribed a copy of his

Jelly Roll Morton recording in 1939. Photograph by Otto Hess?

Mister Jelly Roll for presentation to Carew: "Now I can't wait to see your book on Jelly Roll." Following Carew's death in 1967, Russell received the Carew-Morton correspondence and musical arrangements from the Tempo Music Publishing Company. Using this material as a core, Russell began his own exhaustive research and completed the project in January 1992.

Russell was never close to Morton, but Jelly Roll represents a vital thread running through his entire career as a jazz collector. It was Morton's "Shoe Shiner's Drag" that first sparked his interest in New Orleans style, and it was Morton who became the focus of his early record collecting. Through the research for his book on Jelly Roll, Russell explored the early days of New Orleans jazz. He traced Morton's footsteps as Jelly Roll brought New Orleans style to towns along the Gulf Coast, then further away to Memphis and St. Louis. He examined Morton's glory years in California and Chicago and his fall into obscurity as musical fashions changed. Russell had a genuine respect for Morton's music and his role in the creation of jazz. He was that "someone" Roy Carew was looking for, someone who had "a real regard for [Morton], and for his music."

—Mark Cave

Louis Armstrong, publicity photograph, ca. 1931

LP
33⅓

FOND
MEMORIES

AMERICAN MUSIC
NEW ORLEANS

LOUIS ARMSTRONG

Louis "Satchmo" Armstrong (1901-1971) was born in New Orleans and received his first music lessons in 1913 when he lived in the Colored Waifs' Home. He joined Kid Ory's band in 1918 and Fate Marable's riverboat band before leaving New Orleans in 1922 to join King Oliver's Creole Jazz Band in Chicago. In New York, Armstrong switched from cornet to trumpet and started to appear as a soloist, as well as a singer. When he returned to Chicago in 1925, he was an established star. He recorded with the Hot Five, later the Hot Seven; these recordings are classics in the development of jazz. Armstrong made the first of many European and world tours in 1934 and began to appear in films. By the end of his career, he was one of the world's best-known jazz musicians and a goodwill ambassador for the United States.

LOUIS ARMSTRONG

America's Greatest Trumpet Player

AND HIS ORCHESTRA

Opening Friday, January 28th

WITH AN ALL NEW REVUE

EARLY RESERVATIONS SUGGESTED

probably 1938

Flyer for nightclub table

LOUIS ARMSTRONG

A bout 1935, William Russell began to acquire every record Louis Armstrong made, and then worked with other collectors to compile the first complete discography. Reflecting his admiration for the musician, in 1937 Russell composed a trumpet concerto based on a descending three-note motif found in Armstrong's 1929 OKeh recording of "That Rhythm Man." But it was not until 1939, after Frederic Ramsey, Jr., and Charles Edward Smith asked Russell to write a chapter on Louis Armstrong for their book *Jazzmen* that a personal relationship developed between Russell and Armstrong.

Jazzmen was the foundation of their friendship. Armstrong considered the book to be one of the finest gifts he had ever received. "And many thanks for the Story you wrote about me in *Jazzmen*. Your Kindness shall never be oblibberated," he wrote to Russell in October 1939.

Although there are numerous Armstrong recordings, photographs, and clippings in the William Russell Jazz Collection, possibly the most revealing information comes from letters and from Russell's interview notes and observations. Here is the irrepressible Armstrong in his own words — exuberant, kind, and serious about business.

After receiving a copy of *Jazzmen*, Armstrong wrote Russell on October 3, 1939, "I started to reading it right away and honest — ever since I started to reading that book, I just can't keep my 'Big Head — out of it Ha Ha." He goes on to say that "I defy anybody to even try to 'Borrow it from me." Armstrong tried his best to obtain copies for fans and friends. In September 1942 he wrote, "Now Papa Russell I want you to attend to this for me right away because the young lady's getting ready to go [into] the Army and she wants to take this book with her. On the Firing Line or etc, if necessary. She's just a young 'Fan — and really appreciates, music and its makers, and the night we played at Sioux City there was another young Fan there with one of your books of Jazzmen for me — and I autographed it and the minute this little girl saw it she said — Gee Wiz — (as If to say) I wished I could get one. And right away — Mee — Ol Soft Hearted 'Hatchetmouth' — said — 'Er' wa — Well if you really want one of those books — Why'er — I'll write my boy Bill Russell (AHEM) — familiarity — tee hee not knowing whether you really had one in your possession or not, ha ha. Now Pops — we've got to find a Jazzmen Book from somewheres for the kid. Even if we'll have to buy one from the store. . . . So Papa Russ, Dig this for me wilya? Here the autograph from me to her. All you have to do is to insert it in the book and Lay it on her for me. And then send me the Bill. Hear? I'll pay it with pleasure. And heres, thanking you in advance. You're my boy anyway."

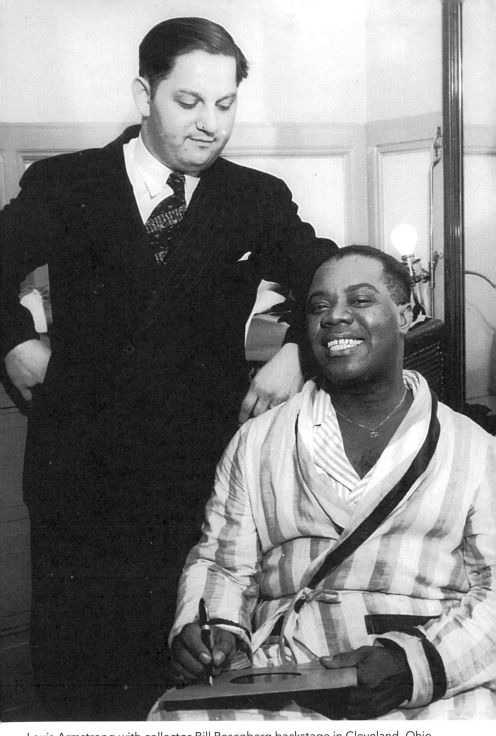

Louis Armstrong with collector Bill Rosenberg backstage in Cleveland, Ohio, 1940 or 1941

Bill Russell, LaVonne Tagge, Louis Armstrong, and George Tagge at the Blue Note, Chicago, November 29, 1954. The Tagges were jazz fans who corresponded frequently with Russell.

To Bill Russe
My Man
Best Wishes
Louis Armstrong

Clarinetist Barney Bigard told Russell, "His heart is so big he'd give anything he had to anyone, and everyone can take advantage of him." Armstrong understood the importance of pleasing people. He knew that to survive in the entertainment industry and to earn a living playing his trumpet he had to give the public what they wanted — he played the tunes they wanted to hear — even if some jazz fans were critical. He was just as generous in giving autographs. Russell's notes from a visit with Armstrong on November 29, 1953, describe Armstrong backstage: "Louis had been sitting with his torso bare, in his dressing room. He put on a sport shirt with the tails out, short sleeved, with pastel green and tan squares. His Chinese food was brought to him right in the paper bucket, and his man set down a bottle of beer and filled a glass. Louis sat on the edge of the raised drum stand, pushing the bass viol out of his way to sign the pictures. There he stayed for nearly two hours, starting to eat the food only after it had gotten cold."

With Armstrong music came first. When Russell asked Armstrong, "How long since you've had a vacation?" Armstrong replied, "Never thought anything about a vacation. I'm always travelin', always new places, lots of fine things." "Is music hard work?" Russell inquired. "Not for me it isn't," Louis answered. "Get so many kicks." This is not to say Armstrong did not work hard at playing his horn. He worked constantly. "If I ever hit a wrong note," he stated, "it's a act of God."

One night in July 1954, jazz record collector Larry Mallory joined Russell and Armstrong in Armstrong's dressing room at the Blue Note in Chicago. Mallory compared the different breaks various New Orleans musicians received, noting how some never seemed to get anyplace. Armstrong replied that some New Orleans guys did not work at things hard enough, didn't keep at it, didn't like one-nighters, didn't want to travel, and sometimes were drunk. Russell once asked Louis if he objected to drinking in his band. Louis replied, "I don't tell them anything. If they can play, I don't care what they do. But they can't play if they're drunk." Another time after relating a story of Baby Dodds being drunk Louis stated, "A musician should drink when he's through work or maybe before he comes to work if he can get a nap in between. He should not drink on the job. It makes it too hard for him to keep that beat going."

Armstrong took music seriously. He informed Russell that sometimes musicians who worked with him did not understand his all-business attitude when he stepped out on the bandstand. "It's all music with me" was how Louis put it.

If he was serious with musicians, his jovial nature shone with friends backstage. In February 1954, Russell and trumpeter Natty Dominique paid Armstrong a backstage visit. After their initial greeting, Louis performed an imitation of Natty being caught unaware as the curtain rose, using his handkerchief as the curtain. Russell remarked that it was one of the funniest impersonations he ever saw. Then Natty demonstrated what would happen if Louis tried to stand up straight and click his heels together. Shortly it was time to get serious again. Russell noted, "As usual Louis warmed up for 15 minutes before the show, at first in his dressing room then down backstage, playing a few numbers, with the stage band."

Russell observed Louis Armstrong's performance at the Blue Note on July 17, 1954. "For the last set or two when he'd stomp off he'd do as I saw him 20 years before, he'd start from over in front of the bass and run toward the back of stage, counting off 1, 2, 3, 4 as he ran. When it was time for each set to start Louis was usually the first one on stand and used his trumpet to call the band. In the middle of the number before time for Velma [Middleton, Armstrong's singer], he pointed his horn toward the dressing room, and in a sort of 'half-valve' way called 'Come here Velma.' Then during a bass solo when Trummie [Young, trombonist] left stand and didn't get back in time he called 'Trum-mie.' "

Always on the road, Armstrong did not have much time for personal correspondence. His letter to Russell, dated September 25, 1942, opened with "I've done things a lots o times and I've done them in a Hustle But I break my neck almost every time To write to my boy — Wm Russell." He goes on to write, "!Man — you talking about a Cat thas, been trying his damdest to get this fine chance to write to you my friend it was Mee. My' Gawd. I never thought that one man could be as busy as your boy Ol Satchmo Gatemouth Louis Armstrong

Louis Armstrong, publicity photograph inscribed to Hoyte Kline, Russell's friend and fellow collector, ca. 1940

Louis Armstrong in Zurich, Switzerland, fall 1949

Lil Armstrong, former wife of Louis Armstrong, and Armstrong in his dressing room, Paris, 1953. Photograph by Hervé Derrien

ha ha But Ah Wuz! ha ha." Russell treasured the letters from Louis and told his friend, "No matter what you do: play, sing, act or write, you're on top for my money."

If there was a shadow over the friendship between Armstrong and Russell, it was cast by Russell's devotion to Bunk Johnson. Louis had informed Russell in an interview for *Jazzmen* that the man he should be talking to was Bunk Johnson in New Iberia, Louisiana. Russell developed a deep admiration for Bunk and when he compared the two musicians, Armstrong did not come out ahead. But Louis's friendship for Russell remained steadfast. On announcing his upcoming marriage to Lucille Wilson, Armstrong wrote, "And if Lucille and I have more than one Satchmo — I'll name one of them Russell. Your Name. Nice? You see the first one will have to be named — Satchmo Louis Armstrong Jr. Savy? ha ha And believe me Pal — we're really going to get down to real — Biz'nez this time. Catch on? Oh Boy."

Russell's last interview with Armstrong, on May 5, 1970, was about Jelly Roll Morton. Louis did not have much to say on the phone that day but, always willing to help, he told Russell to send him a questionnaire in the mail which he would fill out and return. Before hanging up, he said, "I'm glad to hear your voice, Baby. Fond memories." Conversations with Russell always called up memories for Armstrong — moments he cherished. Such fond memories emerge from the Russell Collection.

—Carol O. Bartels

Bunk Johnson at Shadows-on-the-Teche, New Iberia, Louisiana, July 1948.
Photograph by Sam Hatcher

LP
33⅓

JAZZ
ORIGINAL

AMERICAN MUSIC
NEW ORLEANS

BUNK JOHNSON

William "Bunk" Johnson (1879?1889?-1949) was born in New Orleans, but his birth date is still a matter of controversy among jazz scholars. He acquired his first cornet when he was about eight and began playing professionally as a teenager with Adam Olivier's Orchestra. He claimed to have joined Buddy Bolden's band in 1895 as second cornetist. In New Orleans he played with the Superior Orchestra and the Eagle Band, interspersing those jobs with tours with circus bands and minstrel companies. Johnson began touring south Louisiana in 1914, eventually settling in New Iberia in 1920. Loss of his horn and dental problems effectively ended Bunk's musical career in 1932. Bill Russell's assistance led to the revival of that career beginning in 1939. Before his death in New Iberia a decade later, Bunk Johnson made recordings and performed live nationwide, stimulating a "revival" of New Orleans style jazz.

Bunk Johnson, Chicago, 1947. Photograph by Bud Weil

JAZZ ORIGINAL

BUNK JOHNSON

Finding a trumpet for Bunk Johnson was just one way that
Bill Russell showed his support for the man he considered
a major influence in the development of jazz. Russell led an
effort to raise money for Bunk's dental work (essential for a
cornetist), tirelessly recorded his music, and became a real
friend to the musician. Their friendship is revealed in Russell's
letters from Bunk and other correspondents. Russell's admiration for Bunk's role in the jazz community is illuminated in *Bill
Russell's American Music* and his *New Orleans Style*.

Scholars have expended a great deal of energy research-
ing Bunk's birth date to substantiate his claim of playing second cornet with Buddy Bolden in 1895, as well as the general
chronology of his career. Bunk learned the cornet as a young
boy, could read and arrange music, and played in the Eagle
Band and Superior Orchestra, among others. He also toured
with circus orchestras and minstrel shows. After leaving New
Orleans in 1914, he toured south Louisiana, settling in
New Iberia in 1920. There he married Maude Fortinet and
continued to play in local clubs. He also worked in the rice and
sugarcane industries and as a WPA music teacher. The need
for dentures, combined with the destruction of his cornet
in a music hall fight, brought his musical career to a halt in

1932. He worked for artist Weeks Hall at his family estate, Shadows-on-the-Teche, in New Iberia and became popular with the many literary and artistic figures who visited there.

Despite the questions about Johnson's date of birth, Russell believed that Johnson's music was a link to the early style of jazz. Russell constantly recorded the sounds of jazz, perhaps fearing that later music historians would not do the art form justice. The limitations of recorded music, even with technological advances, are evident to anyone who has attended a live performance. Russell probably counted on the possibility that jazz recordings would be refined in the future. He identified Bunk's music as some of the most authentic early jazz worthy of preserving and exerted strenuous efforts to revive Bunk's career as a musician.

Russell became acquainted with Bunk Johnson's work in 1938 and 1939 while interviewing musicians for his chapters in *Jazzmen*, one of the first books on jazz. Notes from interviews with several musicians contain positive comments about Bunk, including an impressive tribute by Louis Armstrong in January 1939: "The fellow they ought to write about is Bunk. Man, what a man! They should talk about that man. How I used to follow him around. Parades. Funerals. He could play funeral marches that would make you cry. . . . His tone! His fingering! Man, what a tone he had! He used his hand like I do." Russell commented, "There was just nobody like Bunk, to hear Louis talk." Although others were more critical, Russell believed in

Bunk Johnson at a radio broadcast in San Francisco, 1942. Photograph by
W. T. O'Dogherty

Bunk Johnson at Jimmy Ryan's, New York City, spring 1945. Band members include trombonist Georg [sic] Brunis, clarinetist Sidney Bechet, and drummer George Wettling. Photograph by Harry Kimon

Bunk Johnson (left), Gene Williams?, and George Lewis (right) in New York City, fall 1945. Photograph attributed to Bill Russell

Bunk's talent and saved letters and articles by his musical peers that confirmed this belief.

A lifelong correspondence began shortly after the Armstrong interview. Bunk's salutations in letters evolved from a generic "Dear Friend" and "Dear Kind Friend" to a very genuine and familiar "Dear Bill." Russell, who respected and befriended Johnson, often helped him financially as well. In a letter to Russell dated February 28, 1939, Bunk expressed regret at not having a photograph to send for inclusion in *Jazzmen*. He mentioned that the reason for his extended hiatus from performing was that he was "in need of a set of teeth."

Bunk wrote Louis Armstrong the next day: "He [Bill Russell]. told. me. that you. all. Had. given. Him. Some. Information. about me." He described his need for dentures and work in the rice and sugarcane industries as a truck driver; he solicited Armstrong's help in getting "Mr. W. R." to pay for six photographs that could be shared with friends. A letter with a cost estimate for dental work was mailed to William Russell in April by Dr. Leonard Bechet, Sidney Bechet's brother, for new teeth. Then followed a letter in May from Fred Ramsey, editor of *Jazzmen* with Charles Edward Smith, expressing impatience about delays in finding an instrument for Bunk and volunteering to join a fundraising effort to speed the process. The team was apparently successful — Bunk acknowledged receiving the requested $25.00 that he used to buy a trumpet and a cornet at "Mr Finks Pond [Pawn] Shop on

South Rampart" in a letter dated September 17, 1939. The seven-month quest brought Bunk from an assortment of odd jobs to the brink of revival.

The start of World War II, which would result in the draft of jazz enthusiasts and limit recording supplies, added pressure to hasten Bunk's promotion and documentation. By March 1942, Gene Williams, editor and publisher of *Jazz Information*, inquired about a better trumpet for Bunk. A letter from record collector Bill Rosenberg to Russell on May 16, 1942, is filled with excitement that a "Selmer, probably the same model that Louis uses" was being sent to Bunk. He also comments on Russell's "very unselfishness and generosity."

One can imagine Russell's satisfaction on receiving Bunk's letter dated May 17, 1942: "It. was. a. real. and. a. great. Pleasure. to. me. when. the. Express. man. brought. that. fine. Selmer. Trumpet. to. me. Saturday. morning. it. Realy. made. me. feel. twenty. years. younger. now. I. am able to Play. you. all. some. Trumpet. and I. can. Realy. go. at. my. age. now. I. am. only. a. real. young. man. and at 62. years. old. and. think. that. the good. good. Lord. will let. me. make. my. other. 62. years. now that. is my Prayer. Every. nite. now. Mr. Russell. You. are. wonderful. and. also. your. good. friend. Mr. Wm. Rosenberg."

In June 1942, Russell finally heard Bunk play in New Iberia. Any uncertainty about Bunk's ability was eliminated, and it was decided that Bunk's music should be recorded. A band of New

Orleans musicians was assembled, but professional studios, following the racial prejudices of the time, would not record the group. A storeroom at Grunewald's Music Store and some borrowed equipment were used to make the first recordings. A follow-up session was recorded at WSMB radio station on Canal Street. By May 1943, Russell acquired recording equipment, which he took to San Francisco where Bunk had gone to perform at the San Francisco Museum of Art. Several records featuring both music and interviews were made under Russell's own American Music label, created in 1944 to market Bunk's work. Russell paid tribute to Johnson by using his three New Iberia addresses as catalogue numbers.

A letter dated September 4, 1943, from jazz enthusiast Ron Stearns suggested the eminent demise of jazz — "the demand and interest in them [jazz records] will slacken and disappear." Such speculations probably strengthened Russell's commitment to record the music. After fifteen months in San Francisco, Bunk returned to New Iberia. In July 1944 he went to New Orleans and recorded in George Lewis's bedroom on St. Philip Street and later at San Jacinto Hall on Dumaine Street.

After a brief and successful performance in New York, Bunk traveled to Boston in April 1945 to play with Sidney Bechet at the Savoy Cafe. He returned to New York in the fall to perform at the Stuyvesant Casino. This appearance generated important media attention that would bring jazz to a new

Bunk Johnson, San Francisco, 1943

Bunk Johnson and Jim Robinson at the Stuyvesant Casino, New York City, 1945 or 1946

generation of fans. Gene Williams acted as Bunk's agent and host while he played in New York. The musician returned to New Iberia and suffered a debilitating stroke in late 1948.

Recording Bunk Johnson's music was part of Russell's lifetime quest to define the elements of jazz. In an article written in 1991, Russell noted that San Francisco jazz collector Bill Colburn believed "that our native music had the power to combat . . . evils and could promote the universal brotherhood of man as well as the pursuit of happiness. . . . Music not only can make people happy but has the power to save civilization." This proposition about the almost spiritual possibilities of music was a component in Russell's fervor.

A letter from Bill Russell's friends Mary and Thurman Grove, written to him in July 1949 shortly after Bunk's death, offers condolences: "Your relationship was one of pure love and mutual admiration. A perfect example of bypassing color boundaries. . . . Your dealings with Johnson are above and beyond such thought. Yours was a sense of helping a friend and a man you admire and his way of playing music you believe in deeply." It must have been a consolation that the recordings he worked so hard to secure would provide supporting evidence for Bunk Johnson's place in the history of jazz.

—M. Theresa LeFevre

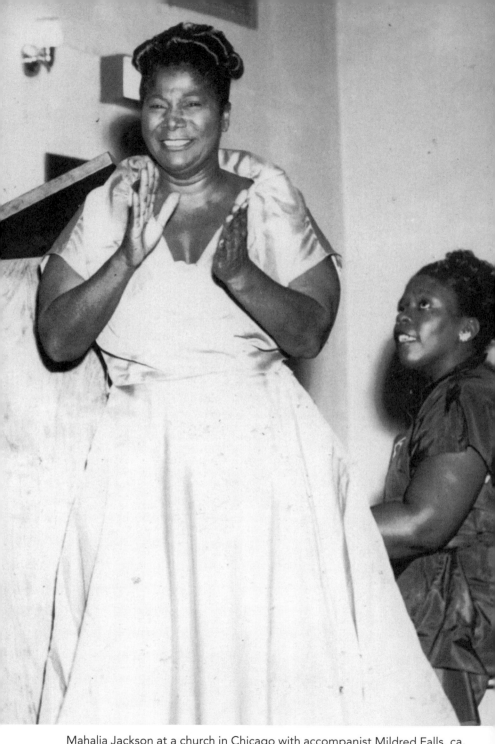

Mahalia Jackson at a church in Chicago with accompanist Mildred Falls, ca. 1954. Photograph by Bill Rosenberg?

LP
33⅓

GOD'S
MUSIC

AMERICAN MUSIC
NEW ORLEANS

MAHALIA JACKSON

Mahalia Jackson (1911-1972) was born in New Orleans and began singing the gospel in her father's church. When she was sixteen, she moved to Chicago to work. She joined the choir of the Greater Salem Baptist Church and later became a member of the Johnson Gospel Singers. Besides radio and television performances, she made many recordings, sang at national religious conventions, and performed at Carnegie Hall. She also appeared at civil rights rallies. When Jackson died, large funerals were held in both Chicago and New Orleans; she is buried in New Orleans. Her signature song was "Move on Up a Little Higher." She won a Grammy in 1976 for "How I Got Over." Among other favorite recordings were "Silent Night," "Nobody Knows the Trouble I've Seen," and "His Eye Is on the Sparrow."

Mahalia Jackson, publicity photograph, ca. 1954

MAHALIA JACKSON

On the last page of one of William Russell's two scrap-books devoted to Mahalia Jackson are photographs he took while they were driving around New Orleans one day in 1954, visiting places from the gospel singer's past. Their friendship blossomed in the 1950s when they both lived in Chicago. Russell frequently visited her home and missed few of her rehearsals or performances.

They visited the house uptown on Water Street where she was born in 1911 and went to Mt. Moriah Baptist Church where her father, a stevedore by day and a barber by night, preached on Sundays. Here, Mahalia first sang religious music.

She described this part of her life: "I gave in to one temptation when I was a child. . . . I disobeyed my parents and listened to the blues, the sorrow songs of my people. I heard the rich, throbbing voices of Ma Rainey, Ethel Waters and Bessie Smith. . . . The inspiration of the church songs, the haunting quality of the work songs and the wail of the blues all got mixed up together in my brain." However, in a later interview, she was quick to point out, "Just remember, all I'm saying about my listening to Bessie and imitating her when I was a little girl, just remember this was before I was saved."

A visit to the house of a friend with several cats sparked

childhood memories. She recalled her pets, a large menagerie that included "several dogs, & a cat, & the polly [parrot], & a couple of goats. Of course they [made] the goats work some. They hitched them up to the wagons when they had to haul things." In the car, on the way home, she talked of the ball games she attended as a girl. Russell recorded that she "belonged to the Black Bloomer Girls, & they played a lot of games. M. could pitch or catch . . . or play 3rd base, or just about any position."

At thirteen, Mahalia wanted to study nursing, but economic realities forced her to go to work. She left New Orleans for Chicago when she was sixteen to find better opportunities. Living with relatives, she worked in factories and as a hotel maid; she also joined her church choir.

As she recalled in later years: "I joined the Greater Salem Baptist church. One Sunday at choir rehearsal, I sang so loud it drowned out the other 49 voices. I got that from David of the Bible. Remember what he said? Sing joyfully unto the Lord with a loud voice. I took his advice."

Her singing began to attract crowds, and she received offers to sing at other churches and in nightclubs. She refused the club offers. Despite her early love of the blues, Mahalia made a vow not to sing them. In 1951, she told *Bronzeville*, "When a man sings the blues and his last note is sung, he is still lonely, still unhappy. There is hope in God's music. There is despair in the blues. . . . I still need

Mahalia Jackson's birthplace, Water Street near the levee, uptown
New Orleans, May 15, 1954. Photograph by Bill Russell

the hope and happiness God's music brings."

While she kept this vow in public, she broke it at least once in private. On May 5, 1955, Russell reported that they were in a car with Mahalia's accompanist Mildred Falls, who mentioned Ella Fitzgerald saying that she once heard her sing Sugar Blues good.

"[Mahalia] said she never paid attention to people singing the Sugar Blues these days, She'd heard the [Blues] really sung, by people like Ida Cook, Ethel Waters. . . . Anyway she (Mahalia) could sing the Sugar Blues, & to prove it she sang a little of it (not more than a line or so) as we drove along on Mich. Ave., thru the loop."

She saved money from her many jobs to pay for education. She studied to be a beautician (which she considered the next best thing to nursing), and opened a beauty shop as well as a florist's shop in Chicago. Although Jackson first recorded gospel material in 1934, she did not become known to the general public until 1945, when her recording of "Move on Up a Little Higher" became a bestseller outside gospel circles.

In the mid-1950s Russell spent a great deal of time with Mahalia, meticulously recording the events of each day in his journals. These center on *Mahalia Sings*, her 1954-55 national radio show and Chicago television show. A look at two days in Russell's journal gives a snapshot of Mahalia's life at that time.

On October 14, 1954, Russell went to Mahalia's house in the evening. As usual, she had several guests, including a visit-

Mahalia Jackson, May 11, 1954, at 1719 Joliet Street, New Orleans, where she later stayed for her brother's funeral. Photograph by Bill Russell

ing preacher. Mahalia was disturbed by an unsigned note, claiming to be "from some colored person who knew her." The writer was offended by the way she talked on her program, and asked "For God's sake and the sake of the race, cut out the dis & dat. Be natural, & as [intelligent] as you are." She was upset enough to have Russell call Studs Terkel, the show's writer. "She wondered if they should have her talk at all, if they'd cut out some of the talking there would be room for another song, or perhaps all they need have her talk would be to read some Bible verses or something."

Thomas A. Dorsey had sent a package of songs for her to rehearse. Dorsey, Ma Rainey's former accompanist, music director of a large Chicago church, and a gospel songwriter, had recognized Mahalia's talent when she sang at his Pilgrim Baptist Church in her teens. While rehearsing Dorsey's songs, accompanist Mildred Falls worried that the show's music director would once again get angry at Mahalia and her musicians "about changing the chords etc. & also not playing them like the [original] was written." The visiting minister "fell asleep on the sofa. For awhile he snored so loud we could hardly hear to rehearse."

Studs Terkel had suggested in the script that Mahalia should sing *a cappella*, with each musician joining in as he was introduced. The next day at the show's taping, Mahalia found this difficult and "explained she needed some support to have any beat. . . . Studs said well it was a good idea on the typewriter."

Recalling the previous evening's critical note, Russell records, "Her 1st take M. had worried about pronouncing the 'sure,' sometimes starting out with 'Sho' and then 'correcting' it to sure. But for her retake, alone, she sang out fully, with more spirit & never once the 'Sure.'"

Mahalia's sudden lack of confidence seems incompatible with her public assuredness. Both qualities are seen in incidents in Russell's journal. On May 21, 1955, Russell notes that "M. went to bed, after having me put on Dr. Kremer's tape (talk for her to give her confidence etc.)." Mahalia claimed her power came from God, and another incident a few days earlier makes it clear how literally she meant this.

On May 12, Russell was watching television with Mahalia, and she began talking about a former gospel singer, Robert Bradley. "He was best singer, & best gospel singer she ever heard." However, he left gospel behind and "all he wanted to sing was operatic stuff." When Mahalia saw him in London in 1952, "It looked like he was ashamed or wanted to get away from the music of his own people. M. told him that as a result God took the power away from him & gave more to her." On another occasion, Mahalia told Russell "she didn't know any-thing about music & (fancy singing – words to that effect) & maybe she didn't sing right etc. & they might find fault with somethings but she knew she could tell the story of the gospel & she could sing about that & no one could take that away from her."

In looking at the clippings from this same time, it becomes clear why Mahalia was so concerned about her image. In 1954 she was both a racial role model and trailblazer. Profiles in African American publications stressed the hard work that went into her success and rarely failed to mention her success as a businesswoman and real estate investor.

Mahalia was also a pioneer within the churches, bringing her knowledge of the blues into religious music. In Russell's entry for July 5, 1955, titled "Mahalia and Hamp at So. Shore Bap. Church," he tells of Lionel Hampton performing at the church at her invitation. As Mahalia told the congregation during the collection, they should give more money because, "If you went to the Blue Note, it would cost you $2."

This sort of event earned her both criticism and praise in gospel circles. That evening Mahalia faced the issue head on, telling the gathering, "some people criticize you for bringing jazz into church but I like it." She also believed it was "alright if the Devil wants to use the Lord's music, such as Closer Walk & Saints." Mahalia knew that her fans would only allow her to go so far in using secular music. "She said the world has so many ways of tempting people, & the church people would be down on her if she did other things."

Russell's role in Mahalia Jackson's life was varied. He was a trusted friend and advisor, but in his careful records, one sees that he often was something of an errand boy. He did some of her gardening and emptied her mousetraps. At rehearsals, he

Mahalia Jackson at 1719 Joliet Street, New Orleans, May 11, 1954.
Photograph by Bill Russell

Mahalia Jackson with Mildred Falls in Chicago, ca. 1954. Photograph by Bill Rosenberg?

was sent out to get her a hamburger or coffee or Kleenex, the prices of which he carefully noted so he could be paid back later. Before rehearsals, he frequently made cue cards of the lyrics of the songs she was to sing. The cards in the Historic New Orleans Collection's William Russell Jazz Collection include such standards as "Nobody Knows the Trouble I've Seen" and "In That Great Gettin' Up Morning."

Perhaps Mahalia should be allowed to sum this up. Russell writes that during a revival at which she sang, "she introduced several people . . . including me, saying I followed her around everyplace & was helpful, that I was 'from the other race but you wouldn't know it.'"

—Nancy Ruck

Baby Dodds playing the snare drum, ca. 1953

LP
33⅓

THE
SHIMMY

AMERICAN MUSIC
NEW ORLEANS

BABY DODDS

Warren "Baby" Dodds (1894-1959) was born in New Orleans and died in Chicago. An exceptional drummer, he studied and played with many of the musicians involved in the early development of jazz. After moving to Chicago in 1921, he played and recorded with other important jazz musicians — King Oliver, Louis Armstrong, Sidney Bechet, and Jelly Roll Morton. In the 1940s he recorded with Bunk Johnson in New Orleans at Bill Russell's behest; he also played in New Orleans, New York, and Europe. Because of his many appearances on classic jazz recordings, Baby Dodds was one of the most influential of the New Orleans style musicians.

Baby Dodds, 1953. Photograph attributed to Bill Russell

BABY DODDS

Bill Russell, who had been seeking out pioneer jazz musicians, first saw Baby Dodds, the drummer from New Orleans, at the Three Deuces in Chicago where Dodds had begun a stint in 1936. Russell wrote: "The first time I ever heard Baby Dodds drum he was playing all by himself on a high bandstand back of the bar at the 222 on Chicago's N. State Street. It was in the middle of the depression, prohibition was gone, but the syndicate mob still ruled the city. The downstairs former speakeasy had been famous for its music in the roaring 20s and now it was again featuring the jazz it helped introduce to the Chicago of Al Capone."

"Only a three-piece New Orleans group was employed." Russell continued, "When I walked in the Deuces that summer nite it was interview time, but not for Baby — he wouldn't quit. Music was fun, he lived to drum; how could he get tired of playing and hearing music. So there he was having the time of his life, all smiles his face glowing doing his 'shimmy,' his consciousness lost in the beauties of the tone and intricate rhythms that rolled from his relaxed hands and feet (a cascade of beautiful sounds and tantalizing rhythms that poured out of his drums and traps.) When this (cascade) was over Baby sang a specialty of his 'Big Butter and Egg Man' and accompanied himself on drums (a most delicate and varied accompaniment)."

William Russell wrote about the difficulties of Baby's career: "Life had been tough in New Orleans too, scrounging for vegetables and fruit back of the French Market and wharves along the Mississippi and later working in a burlap factory to earn a living and buy his first drum set. Only a dozen years had lapsed since Baby had drummed for Louis Armstrong, Jelly Roll, and King Oliver, but it must have seemed like an eternity, what with few jobs, missed meals and loss."

Warren Dodds was born in New Orleans on Christmas Eve 1894. Because he was the youngest child at the time — and his father was also named Warren — his mother started calling him "the baby" to distinguish between father and son, and the nickname stuck.

Dodds became interested in music at an early age but could not afford the flute he wanted to play. He was envious of his brother Johnny, who played clarinet around the neighborhood, entertaining at parties on Sundays for ice cream and cake. To get in on the act, he made drums out of lard cans, using spindles from his mother's chairs for sticks.

At sixteen, he worked for a wealthy family doing a

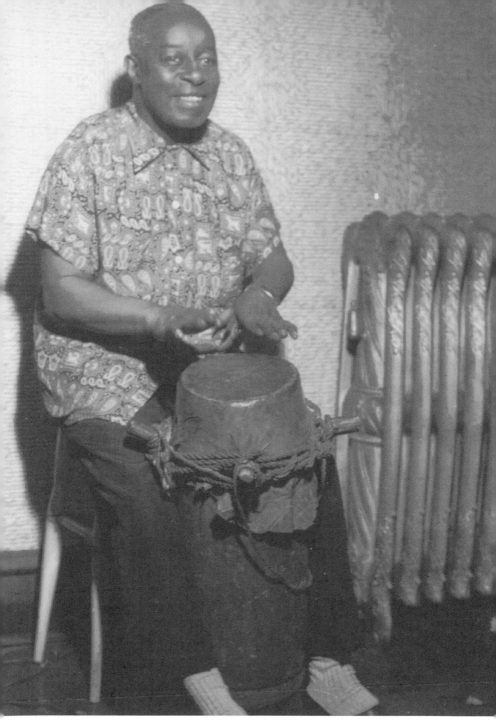

Baby Dodds, playing homemade drum, ca. 1953

variety of household chores, saving enough money to buy his first snare drum. Baby then took a better paying job at a burlap sack factory that allowed him to purchase the rest of his drum set, including a bass drum, cymbal, and wood block, as well as a ratchet and whistles.

After taking lessons from New Orleans drummers Dave Perkins, Walter Brundy, and Louis Cottrell, Baby worked with Willie Hightower's American Stars at the Fewclothes Cabaret downtown. Sometimes he played with Manuel "Fess" Manetta at the Casino Cabaret, Frankie Duson's Eagle Band — Bunk Johnson and Papa Celestin were among the musicians — and in various brass bands around New Orleans. During this time he developed his "shimmy" technique of shaking his entire body while playing.

In late 1918 Pops Foster got Baby a job with Fate Marable's band on the Streckfus line of riverboats. Another band member was Louis Armstrong. Both Dodds and Armstrong quit in 1921 because of differences with the bandleader concerning proper rhythm. About this time, King Oliver lost his drummer and wanted Baby Dodds as a replacement. Baby's brother Johnny Dodds, who played clarinet in the Oliver band, said that Baby drank too much and wasn't good enough. But Davey Jones, Marable's saxophonist, told Oliver that Baby was just as big a drawing card as Louis Armstrong.

Baby joined King Oliver in San Francisco; in 1922 the band — and Baby — left for Chicago. Louis Armstrong, who was still in New Orleans when Oliver asked him to join the group, said, "I got to go. Man, Baby Dodds is drumming with King Oliver." They played at the Lincoln Gardens and recorded for the Gennett, Paramount, and Columbia labels until a financial dispute broke up the band in 1923.

Baby Dodds remained in Chicago for the next dozen years, playing with various bands and recording with Armstrong, Jelly Roll Morton, and his brother Johnny. In 1927, Dodds played drums for many of Louis Armstrong's Hot Seven recordings as well as for Jelly Roll Morton's Red Hot Peppers recordings. Concerning these years in Chicago Bill Russell wrote, "Drummers still came in to learn and be inspired by Baby and stories are still told of the nights Gene Krupa, then touring with Benny Goodman, and other nationally known drummers dropped in the Deuces to get their lessons from Baby."

After continuing to play around Chicago in the early 1940s, Dodds returned to New Orleans several times in 1944 and 1945 at the request of Bill Russell to record with a band featuring Bunk Johnson. Bunk was on trumpet; George Lewis on clarinet; Jim Robinson, trombone; Lawrence Marrero, banjo; Slow Drag Pavageau, bass; and Baby on drums. Dodds also recorded with other

New Orleans musicians in bands of various configurations, with many of the recordings taking place at George Lewis's home at 827 St. Philip Street as well as at San Jacinto Hall and Artisan Hall.

When he returned to New Orleans to see Russell, Dodds seemed excited about being there. Recalling their conversation, Russell said: "Then Baby got serious for a few minutes and told how all his family had died young and how he didn't expect to live long. When talking, his actions and movements were remarkable; not only were they very rhythmic and dynamic but the looseness and control of all his muscles and entire body was really something to marvel at. I had no worries about how he would play with a 'real New Orleans band' after all these years."

Dodds made his first trip to New York in 1945 to play with Bunk Johnson's group at the Stuyvesant Casino. There were other trips to New York and one to Europe in 1948 with a band led by Mezz Mezzrow. Although Baby suffered a stroke in 1949, he still made trips to New York to play at Jimmy Ryan's.

Between 1952 and 1954, Bill Russell recorded twelve reels of interviews and drum demonstrations with Baby Dodds. Some of this material was released on three American Music LPs. A fourth LP, planned but never released, was to accompany an instruction booklet on

Baby Dodds and clarinetist George Lewis at Lewis's home, 827 St. Philip Street, New Orleans, August 1944. Photograph attributed to Bill Russell

Baby Dodds at a recording session for the Art Hodes Trio, November 1953

drumming and a 16-mm film. Russell's book *New Orleans Style* included a chapter on Dodds, based on these interviews. Russell thought highly of Baby's technique — the early New Orleans jazz style — but he also appreciated the emotional impact of his drumming. Russell made this notation: "Everyone who speaks of Baby Dodds, anyone who ever heard him, ever saw him, remembers/thinks 1st of his happy face, transformed/transfigured with joy of making music his whole body possessed with happy rhythm. How could such a person fail to (diffuse) rhythm & inspire & fire any band with whom he played. How could any audience, listener or drummer fail to gain new hope & a happier outlook/spirit on life (when set in motion, when turned into this dynamo of rhy[thm] & happiness), come away with a new outlook on life, their mind & body rejuvenated."

Firmly rooted in traditional jazz, Dodds disdained modern styles. "Well," said Baby, "bop is like a man who sits down to write a letter and never finishes a sentence. . . . The drum is not just something to beat; it's the timepiece of the orchestra. The drum should be felt, not heard. It's just noise the way they do it now."

In a face-off with bebop drummer Max Roach in the 1940s, Baby followed a wild and intricate solo by Roach. Max recalls, "Baby just reached for his snare drum. The snare vibrates, you know. And all he did was blow on it.

Baby Dodds, ca. 1953

That sound, that sound said more than all the pyrotechnics I was doing. It was so human, I learned a lot that day."

Ironically, Baby was sometimes accused of being too loud and showy himself. Bunk Johnson thought so. And drummer George Wettling said, "The way he played drums behind the band was a solo in itself."

According to Bill Russell, Baby was the most influential of all New Orleans drummers because of his wide travels and extensive recordings with King Oliver, Louis Armstrong, Jelly Roll Morton, Bunk Johnson, and other well-known musicians. Russell wrote, "Baby's lifetime of happy and inspired playing demonstrated that a drummer can be as great a musician as any other instrumentalist. Baby was a wonderful talker and thinker on the problems of the drummer and his place in the band."

In spite of poor health — Dodds was a heavy drinker — he continued to play occasionally until 1957. He died in Chicago in 1959, shortly before his autobiography, *The Baby Dodds Story* (as told to Larry Gara), was published. His friends wanted to give him a traditional New Orleans brass-band funeral, but they were unable to muster enough musicians. Natty Dominique said, "There just aren't enough of us around from New Orleans any more. Three or four, and that ain't enough."

—Dan B. Ross

Natty Dominique, Chicago, 1952. Photograph attributed to George Kinney

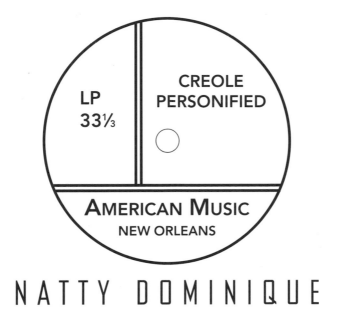

LP
33⅓

CREOLE
PERSONIFIED

AMERICAN MUSIC
NEW ORLEANS

NATTY DOMINIQUE

Natty Dominique (1894-1982) was born Anatie Dominique in New Orleans. Initially trained to play drums, he turned to the trumpet as a teenager. He moved to Chicago with his family in 1913, where he eventually played professional music full time, appearing on Jelly Roll Morton's first band recording. During the 1920s and 1930s he played with various Chicago and touring bands but was regularly associated with Johnny Dodds's band. Disappointed with the sounds of modern jazz, Dominique left the profession for awhile during the 1940s, working as an airport redcap. He returned to professional music by the early 1950s, soon leading his own traditional New Orleans style band.

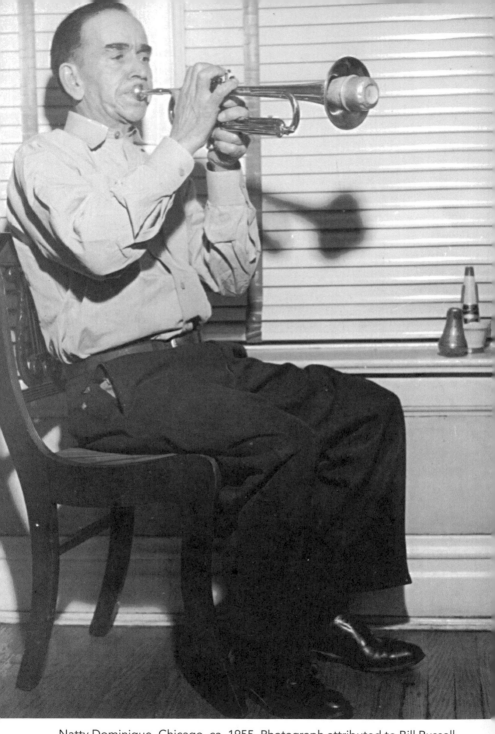

Natty Dominique, Chicago, ca. 1955. Photograph attributed to Bill Russell

NATTY DOMINIQUE

His given name was Anatie Dominique, but most people called him Natty as an adult. In an interview with his friend Bill Russell, he recalled that he got his nickname from big band leader Paul Whiteman at the K-9 Club in Chicago where he played for a spell in the 1920s. "To Hell with that Anatie," Whiteman quipped, "I'm gonna call you Natty."

Dominique was born in New Orleans on August 2, 1894, according to his own reckoning. For some reason, Russell believed that the musician was younger, writing in biographical sketches that his birth date was either 1895 or 1896. While remembered as a trumpet player, Natty began by playing drums when he was about thirteen or fourteen years old, switching to the cornet at fifteen. Rather than going to his first horn lesson, however, the teenager played marbles. His instructor, Manuel Perez, picked him up and kept him at the Perez house all evening before he started the lesson. Russell reported that "Natty didn't get home until late . . . . So he got a good licking from his dad."

Dominique was apprenticed young to one of the city's many cigar makers. But he also played with jazz bands at various "halls and places," including Hopes Hall, St. Katherine's

Hall, and the Milneburg amusement park. He moved with his family to Chicago, arriving July 27, 1913. The city remained his home until his death on August 30, 1982.

Before settling into his career as a Chicago musician, he spent some time as a cigar maker in Canada, later instructing Bill Russell in the finer techniques of rolling a cigar. While in Canada he improved his French: his fluency combined with his light complexion prompted Louis Armstrong to say of Natty to Bill Russell, "There's Creole personified."

Back in Chicago, he worked at an array of clubs over the years including Kelly's Stables. There he replaced Freddy Keppard as trumpet player in 1925 — even though Keppard warned the light-skinned Natty that "he wasn't dark enough to make a t[rum]p[e]t player." Dominique reminisced that Kelly's Stables, "was painted black inside & people used to scratch their names on the wall. It really was nothing but a dump, but people who came from Russia & all over the world wanted to see it."

Another Windy City club where Dominique played was the Sunset; there he worked with Louis Armstrong. During the 1930s Dominique worked with the Dodds brothers — Johnny and Baby — but he left full-time music in the early 1940s, working as a redcap at Midway Airport in Chicago. In an unidentified magazine article from about 1950 written by J. Lee Anderson, Dominique was quoted as saying, "If and when they make it worth my while, I'll be back playing music." In

Natty Dominique and Pal, Chicago, January 1956, with Bill Russell's shadow in foreground. Photograph by Bill Russell

Preston Jackson, Jasper Taylor, Natty Dominique, and Odell Rand, Chicago, 1952. Photograph by Ralph Jungheim

1952 he organized what the *Chicago Daily Tribune* described as an "octet of old timers most of whom actually came from New Orleans." He reintroduced the Slow Drag — dubbed "New Orleans's Oldest and Chicago's Newest Rhythm."

Natty preferred New Orleans style jazz which he described as "played in a medium tone," and he disliked loud, modern music. "Bop sounds like a gang of hogs crying for corn," he complained. "There's no melody to bop, just racket, and nobody understands what you're playing." Of a drummer with whom he played in the King Oliver Orchestra at the Dreamland Cafe in Chicago, he commented that, "He played so much loud drums that it gave me the worst headache I ever had in my life . . . with his noise, I would never have him to play in my orchestra as long as I live; not even in my chicken coop or pig pen, because he'd kill them all, like he nearly killed me." In 1955 he lamented, "everybody's making noise nowadays, and think it's jazz."

Nothing in the Dominique correspondence indicates when he and Bill Russell first met, although Russell did interview Dominique, along with other jazzmen, as early as 1938. Personal correspondence in the file consists mostly of letters from Dominique to Russell. Some pages of Russell's interviews with the musician are included, but no letters from him. It is clear from the surviving correspondence, however, that they were friends. Dominique often refers to himself as "your pal" and calls Russell "my Friend," a "real friend," and "my best friend."

Dominique was a loyal and regular correspondent, leaving a trail of letters, postcards, and Christmas cards. Many read the same. One postcard of June 19, 1962, is typical of the others — "Hi! Bill Just a card to let you know wife & I are well hoping you are the same. Lots of Luck in your business tell the gang Hello for me all send best wishes to you your pal Natty Dominique."

Bill Russell was not so reliable, often prompting letters from a worried-sounding Natty. On November 3, 1956, Dominique wrote, "if possible you have any spare time Please answer this letter," followed on January 29, 1957, with, "I am at Baby [Dodds]'s house Why don't you write Baby & Natty We are worried what seem to be the trouble We are waiting to hear from you." Then on April 9 Russell was asked, "I do hope that you would have time to write Baby and I. We know yu [sic] are a busy man. . . .Well all of us are always talking about you how a nice man you are So Bill if you have a little time to Spare drop us a line or two." On June 29, 1970, after having offered Russell an old violin that lacked strings, he wrote, "Bill my Friend I have a Violin th[at] a Janitor gave me I want you to have it I know you can do something with it. this is the 3rd letter I am writing you please answer this one Bill I would like very much to hear from you."

While he may not have written often, Russell was dependable in providing advice and assistance. In 1956 Natty nearly overlooked renewing the copyrights on three of his 1928

Baby Dodds and Natty Dominique, Chicago, ca. 1955

compositions, "Brush Stomp," "Lady Love," and "Sweep 'Em Clean." These could have lapsed, had it not been for Russell and his commitment to helping protect the copyrights of his musician friends — in Russell's book collection there are eight dealing with copyright law. Dominique showed his gratitude in a letter of July 16, 1956, when he wrote, "Had it not been for your watchful eye I would have lost these numbers."

On November 3, 1956, over another copyright issue, Dominique wrote, "I will take your advise. I certainly appreciate all the advise you are giving me," and in the postscript to a letter dated December 6, 1957, he promised, "Bill I will not sign any contract with no publishers I will always consult you before doing anything." Still concerned about his copyrights he wrote on December 27, 1957, "It seems as though they want to take my numbers away from me. Bill I am depending on you please help me I will never forget you pal."

Russell occasionally sent Dominique books as gifts. On August 28, 1965, an excited Dominique wrote, "Bill old friend I cannot get over that book you sent me for my Birthday I am very very happy to know that I have a real good friend." On May 6, 1969, Natty asked Russell if he knew "about that book that is out they tell me my picture and nice write up about me is in this book please write me and let me know if it is true . . . let me know at once." After Russell sent him a copy of the unidentified work, Natty replied on June 7, "Received your letter and the book thanks very very much . . . you are a real friend Bill that is a real Birthday present."

Dominique always maintained his New Orleans associations and his connection with other old-time jazzmen. He recalled that when he first met Jelly Roll Morton in Chicago, Morton said, "I'm from that old crayfish town you come from, but that's a good town, that's a good town." Dominique always found time to ask Russell to remember him to the "gang" in New Orleans, and he must not have lost his taste for New Orleans cooking. In a letter of October 9, 1969, he wrote, "Say Bill do you know any address where I can buy select oysters if you know send me the address because I love Oysters Bill I am crazy about them. you cannot get any good oysters in Chi."

Bill Russell's collected memorabilia and letters about and by his friend Natty Dominique reflect an acquaintance of more than forty years that deepened into a fast friendship by the early 1950s, a relationship that lasted until Dominique's death. Dominique called Russell a "nice man," and the Russell collection makes it clear that they were two of a kind — loyal friends who shared a love for old style jazz.

—John Magill

Fess Manetta, September 1957

LP
33⅓

MAISONS
DE JOIE

AMERICAN MUSIC
NEW ORLEANS

FESS MANETTA

Manuel "Fess" Manetta (1889-1969) was born and died in Algiers, the portion of New Orleans that lies across the Mississippi River. As a professional musician until about 1923, he played violin, piano, and other instruments with such legendary bands as those of Buddy Bolden, Jack Carey, Frank Duson, Kid Ory, and King Oliver, and played piano in the red-light district of New Orleans. After stints on the excursion boat *Capitol* and with Oscar "Papa" Celestin's band, Manetta began teaching various instruments full-time. Like all music "professors" of the day, he was known as "Fess." He continued to appear occasionally in clubs as an entertainer playing two brass instruments simultaneously and in harmony.

Fess Manetta, ca. 1958. Photograph by Richard Tolbert?

FESS MANETTA

"Manetta was a good talker (although very slow), and had a broad knowledge of New Orleans music and musicians," Bill Russell wrote. "[He] was one of the older musicians remaining in the city. . . . So he was interviewed in great depth, and enough material obtained on over 200 tapes and cassette reels to probably fill a full-length autobiography. He was not known widely partly because he only recorded once (on piano) with [Oscar "Papa"] Celestin in the 1920s, and he devoted most of his time to teaching music after 1922 in the little studio by his home, across the river in Algiers. . . .Violin was his first instrument in 1906, but he was best known as a pianist in the District, a few years later."

Here Russell nicely summed up Manetta's career and why he considered the musician important. And he apparently considered him <u>very</u> important, preserving a great number of his effects: dozens of notebooks kept by his students, photographs, clippings about Algiers, clippings about subjects only vaguely related to Manetta, a musical arrangement, even musical instruments he once owned. Then, of course, there are those 200 tapes of interviews. He never did transcribe the Manetta autobiography, but he used a portion of the taped material in his book *New Orleans Style*, published posthumously in 1994.

The "District" was, of course, the red-light district of New Orleans — the famous Storyville — that existed from 1897 until 1917. It was named by the daily press for Alderman Sidney Story, who proposed the ordinance confining prostitution in New Orleans to an area roughly twenty blocks square, just behind the French Quarter, with Basin Street as its lower boundary. Solo musicians, mostly pianists, were hired to perform in the parlors of its dozens of brothels; bands appeared in its numerous cabarets, its five dance halls, and some of its countless saloons.

Pianist/music publisher Clarence Williams, who played in Storyville, left an interesting description of the larger brothels. "Places like that," he said, "were for rich people, [only] white. . . . The customers would buy champagne mostly and would always insist on giving the musicians money. . . . And there was no loud playing either. It was sweet, just like a hotel."

Manetta's introduction to Storyville was as a teenage violinist and occasional pianist, earning about $1.50 an hour when he joined a small band consisting of a guitar, mandolin, and bass. In waiter-style white jackets they played at a saloon at Marais and Iberville Streets. The Manetta family consented to young Manuel's participation because the leader, the bass player, was an old friend. Before his tenure in Storyville ended,

Guitarist/banjoist Johnny St. Cyr and Fess Manetta, Los Angeles,
August 1958

The Original Tuxedo Orchestra, ca. 1924. Fess Manetta is standing, second from right; Oscar "Papa" Celestin seated, second from right.

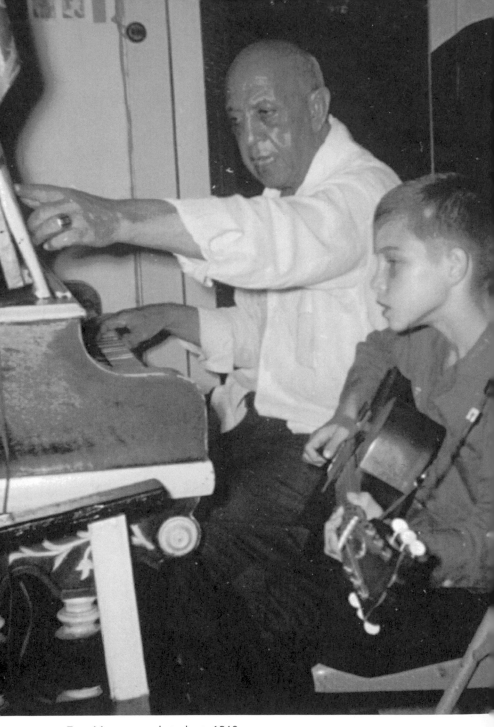

Fess Manetta and student, 1960s

Manetta would be associated with some of the most famous and colorful of its characters.

One day while Manetta was playing with the little band, the Shriners came to town. Their favorite song then, even prior to World War I, was "It's a Long Way to Tipperary." He was demonstrating the song on the piano for the mandolin player, who couldn't read music, when he was heard by "Lulu White's old man," as he put it.

"Listen. How would you like to play a job in a parlor? You wouldn't have to wear no white coat, you could stay dressed," the man suggested.

"When I knocked off," Manetta related to Russell, "and told my family about the offer, they didn't like the idea at first, but I guess they warmed to it, and finally I went to work at Lulu White's." (The reason the poor Manetta family probably "warmed" to the idea was that the money for musicians at the brothels was so good.) "I stayed for over a year and eight months."

Lulu White, the famous Storyville madam, had built a three-story "house" at 235 Basin Street, called Mahogany Hall. She had more than thirty women (all octoroons) working on-call for her in 1900. Besides its principal commodity, Mahogany Hall became so renowned for the quality of its music that Bill Russell preserved fragments of one of its mirrors in his collection when the building was demolished in 1949. Each evening when Manetta climbed the steep steps from the sidewalk, he encountered the fan-shaped window of multi-colored glass over the front door. It held not only the house number but spelled out "Lulu White"; that well-known window is now in the possession of New Orleans clarinetist Pete Fountain.

The African American Lulu White (she told everyone she was West Indian) was widely known for lavish jewelry, including diamond rings on every finger. In fact, she was called the "Diamond Queen." She wore a bright red wig, was said to be short and full-figured ("She had a real large face," reported Manetta gallantly), and had a rather thin, squeaky voice. With her diamonds and her independence, Lulu was an acknowledged model for Mae West.

"At first, when you came in, they had a real plush entry hall," Manetta remembered. "Lulu herself . . . sat to the left of the entry. . . . It looked like a ticket office for a theater but bigger. She would sit there all the time. . . . I played in the parlor on the second floor. They had an upright piano. . . . There was three or four waiters on hand and the girls all wore beautiful costumes and such. Long evening gowns. . . . I started at nine o'clock p.m. and played till three. Sometimes I wouldn't get out of there till nine the next morning, though."

Manetta often made hundreds of dollars a week. The madams would apparently guarantee their piano players a small weekly minimum, but the real money came from the tips of the "johns," encouraged by the girls and, no doubt, the

Lulu White's Mahogany Hall, December 23, 1946, just prior to demolition

Bill Russell and Fess Manetta at Russell's shop, 600 Chartres Street, New Orleans, summer 1958. Photograph by Walter Eyslincyck

liquid refreshments sold in the houses. Manetta told Russell that when his mother saw the money he earned, she "cried with joy."

But despite Manetta's close relationship with Lulu White — they called each other "son" and "mama," and she once gave him one of her diamond rings — the musician eventually lost his job. One busy night he arranged for a substitute piano player while he attended a special boxing match featuring a childhood buddy. When his replacement failed to show up, Fess was fired by Lulu's "old man." The interview doesn't record if this was the same man who hired him.

The chronology is uncertain before and after Manetta left Mahogany Hall. It is probable, though, that he worked as a piano player for one or more of Storyville's other madams, like Pinky on Iberville Street or the Countess Willie V. Piazza in the next block from Lulu White's on Basin Street. As outrageous as Miss Lulu, the Countess Willie wore a monocle, smoked cigarettes in a two-foot long ivory, gold, and diamond holder, and owned a white piano. The most musical of the madams, she had a reputation for keeping her piano tuned.

Manetta as a youngster also played piano in a band led by Papa Celestin at Storyville's Tuxedo Dance Hall on Franklin (now Crozat) Street around the corner from Miss Lulu's. He went to Chicago briefly in 1913 when the Tuxedo was closed for a year after a sensational double murder there. The following year Manetta returned, playing piano for eight or nine

months for Gertrude Dix, Basin Street madam and lover —
later wife — of the incredible Tom Anderson, known as benev-
olent dictator of Storyville. Anderson was a a dashing figure —
a member of the state legislature, a huge Storyville property
owner (his saloon on the corner of Iberville and Basin with its
half-block long bar was world famous), and lover of many
Storyville madams.

"Tom Anderson's son-in-law opened a cabaret on
Rampart. . . . Mr. Anderson, he says 'I want you to go over and
play for him'. . . . so I hired the band myself," Manetta told
Russell. "I stayed on that job for over two years." There were
four instrumentalists, as well as three singers/dancers.

The Dix-Anderson job was apparently Manetta's farewell
to Storyville. Years later, one of his last extensive performing
jobs before settling down to teaching, however, may have
been what endeared him to Russell. Manetta was hired by the
Streckfus family of St. Louis to play piano in the Fate Marable
band on the *Capitol* and to play the ship's calliope, or steam
organ. Manetta pronounced the word "cal'-i-ope" — three syl-
lables with the accent on the first — just as the New Orleans
street of the same name is pronounced by locals.

Writing thirteen years after Manetta's death about a possible Manetta record from a tape he made in 1957, Russell said,
"I'd suggest a very fine little section…where he talks about
playing calliope on the excursion boat and illustrates the style
on his very old studio piano, which he makes sound just

Fess Manetta, trombonist and bandleader Kid Ory, and Ory's daughter at Ory's home north of San Francisco, August 1958

exactly the way they used to play calliope. To me this was a very wonderful little recorded section, but then I'm prejudiced since the calliope was some of the first music I ever heard when I was a kid, or even a baby, and it has always been some of my favorite music. When we were little kids anytime Homer [Russell's brother] and I would hear the calliope we'd run for the river."

In a sense the William Russell Jazz Collection restores to history this one-time Storyville musician, one-time calliope player. Though he lived to be eighty years old, teaching dozens of music students — both black and white — a variety of instruments in his little Algiers studio, until his last days Manetta never forgot his early experiences. The jazz clarinetist and Manetta pupil Albert Nicholas called him "one of the greatest musicians of all time." If this statement is even partly true, the demanding and unpredictable musical work of the early years of the century could only have sharpened his skills.

—Richard Jackson

Bill Russell at the entrance to Preservation Hall, April 1978

THE WILLIAM RUSSELL
JAZZ COLLECTION

Assembled over nearly sixty years, the collection of jazz chron-icler William "Bill" Russell was acquired by the Historic New Orleans Collection in 1992. The cornerstone of the collection is material on Jelly Roll Morton — letters, music manuscripts, photographs, piano rolls, and recordings. Mahalia Jackson, Bunk Johnson, Baby Dodds, Fess Manetta, Louis Armstrong, and Natty Dominique are also represented by substantial holdings, along with Russell's correspondence with hundreds of jazz musicians and early jazz scholars. The collection includes books, ephemera, oral histories, sheet music, photographs, postcards, and recordings that document the development of jazz within the context of the general musical history of New Orleans.

percussion music seattle '38 - nyc '90

the music We
lIked the most
more than anything eLse
the music we Loved
was always anythIng
no mAtter how short   anything you'd writte[n]
what gave us the Most

pleasuRe was
when yoU'ld
write Something new
and now late in my life there'S
a long voodoo ballEt ogou badagri
what an amazing deLight
i can hardLy wait

John Cage

Bill Russell. Photograph by Sabine Mathes. Poem by John Cage.
Courtesy Dr. Don Gillespie, C. F. Peters Corporation

THE WILLIAM RUSSELL JAZZ COLLECTION

B ill Russell, the jazz collector, was an exceptional figure. Described by friends as unpretentious, selfless, and generous, he was a passionate, determined, and relentless collector. Perhaps the secret of his success as a collector was his role as confidant to jazz musicians. He not only collected material about and by jazz greats but knew and assisted them. They were personal friends: he arranged recording sessions and concerts, helped to resolve copyright questions, paid them union scale for interviews, and assisted their widows. The musicians' trust in him is reflected in his collection.

A composer himself, Russell was a pioneer in the integration of African, Caribbean, and Asian instruments with European instruments and found objects. Indeed, his jazz collection reflects his philosophy of composition: the development of a truly independent American art form must draw from the multi-ethnic community that is America.

Distinguished by the friendships he formed with major jazz figures, Russell's collection is also extraordinary in scope. Collectors frequently focus on one particular genre — records, sheet music, photographs. Russell, however, documented jazz in the widest variety of formats, including — but not limited to — books, correspondence, ephemera, musical instruments, music manuscripts, newspaper clippings, oral history, periodicals, photographs, postcards, recordings, and sheet music. Whether in Chicago or the French Quarter of New Orleans, he was constantly in touch with musicians in their milieu, preserving and generating primary sources. His long-term, intimate association with the world of jazz was the source of the comprehensiveness, continuity, and intuitive understanding that are the hallmarks of his collection.

Russell's collection was to some degree a family affair. While he had corresponded with Bunk Johnson in New Iberia for several years, it was his family who first visited Bunk during a New Year's holiday. The collector himself met the musician later. Many of the Chicago photographs of musicians were taken by Russell's brother, William Wagner. While a doctoral student in Chicago, "Brother Bill," as he is still affectionately known, accompanied Russell on record-hunting expeditions in Chicago. They began each day with a bag for records, a few dollars, and some food. When the money and provisions ran out, they returned home. Any appreciation of Russell's collection must include respect for Brother Bill, who faithfully carried out his brother's desire to see that the collection was properly cared for after his death.

A cornerstone of the collection is Jelly Roll Morton. While

Jelly Roll Morton, age 17, believed by Bill Russell to be the earliest photograph of Morton

Bunk Johnson at Jimmy Ryan's, New York City, spring 1945. Photograph by Harry Kimon

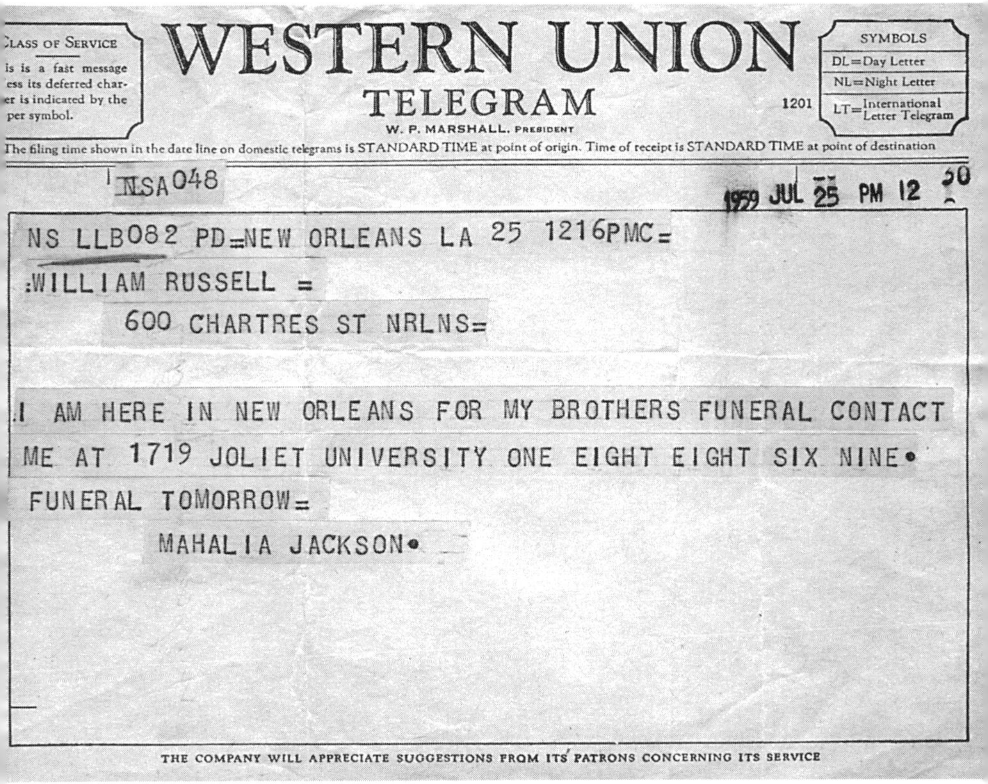

WESTERN UNION

TELEGRAM

W. P. MARSHALL, PRESIDENT

1201

The filing time shown in the date line on domestic telegrams is STANDARD TIME at point of origin. Time of receipt is STANDARD TIME at point of destination

NLSA048

1959 JUL 25 PM 12 50

NS LLB082 PD=NEW ORLEANS LA 25 1216PMC=

:WILLIAM RUSSELL =

600 CHARTRES ST NRLNS=

I AM HERE IN NEW ORLEANS FOR MY BROTHERS FUNERAL CONTACT
ME AT 1719 JOLIET UNIVERSITY ONE EIGHT EIGHT SIX NINE.
FUNERAL TOMORROW=

MAHALIA JACKSON.

Telegram from Mahalia Jackson to Bill Russell, July 25, 1959

Russell's enthusiasm for Jelly Roll is legendary, his personal contact with the pianist was limited. The men met several times, but Jelly died before they could develop a close relationship. The more than two hundred letters from Morton were not acquired from the pianist but from Roy Carew, his publisher. The manuscript music, lyrics, photographs, piano rolls, and published music by Jelly Roll are supplemented by interviews that Russell conducted throughout the United States with Jelly's half-sister and a host of musicians who worked with him — from Eubie Blake to Louis Armstrong.

Russell's quest for musicians associated with the development of early jazz led him to Bunk Johnson, whom he first recorded in 1942. When his attempts to sell the recording to a national distributor failed, Russell founded his own American Music label in 1944. In typical fashion, he purchased photographs, letters, and memorabilia from Johnson's wife Maude. He carefully organized and stored his treasures in plastic bags recycled from the A&P on the corner of Royal and St. Peter Streets. Hidden within other boxes of a more miscellaneous nature were Russell's collection of publicity material on Johnson and other information gathered for his planned "Bunk Book."

The Mahalia Jackson papers reflect Russell's role as her confidant during the early 1950s in Chicago. Carefully recording the expenses he incurred on her behalf, his account book virtually retraces her daily activities. Saved are the cue

Arlington Nite Club, 200 block of Basin Street, New Orleans, 1942. Russell noted on the back, "Checked with Fess." Photograph attributed to Bill Russell

cards for her television shows, as well as stage diagrams. Informal tape recordings of Mahalia in rehearsal provide the connoisseur not with a polished performance, but with a rare glimpse of this giant of gospel music preparing for a performance. After Russell moved to New Orleans, the two remained close. When the singer's brother died, she sent Russell a telegram letting him know of her arrival for the funeral.

Once they toured New Orleans together, visiting sites associated with her youth. Russell photographed everything that sunny day. Later, her funeral cortege would slowly wind uptown from the Rivergate and pass all those places on its way to her final resting place in Providence Memorial Park cemetery. In tribute to their friendship, despite his sadness, Russell dutifully clipped accounts of the funeral for his Mahalia files.

The General Correspondence Files contain Russell's correspondence, clippings, photographs, and ephemera concerning more than 185 musical figures, not all of whom were involved in jazz. Because of his frugal nature (he made notes on the backs of letters after he had drawn a big "X" over the contents), information on his other concerns, from musical composition to the environment and the death penalty, is also preserved. Many notes about jazz musicians appear on the reverse of letters from composers or social activists such as Sister Helen Prejean, author of *Dead Man Walking*, or Jesuit peace crusader Daniel Berrigan. These letters indicate the depth of Russell's other musical and humanitarian interests.

Bill Russell at Economy Hall, longtime jazz site, after Hurricane Betsy, October 1965. Photograph by Allan Jaffe

While not a professional photographer, he recorded many important, now long-vanished sites associated with jazz, as well as other landmarks in his adopted city. In characteristic fashion he photographed oak-lined North Claiborne Avenue before chain saws made way for an expressway and then photographed the construction. His photographs are informal snapshots, capturing such moments as Bunk Johnson and George Lewis relaxing in Gene Williams's kitchen after a performance. His passion for detail is evident: he carefully noted the date, the place, and the individuals in each photograph. Russell maintained separate files for photographs he merely acquired, always identifying the photographer. Like all collectors, he had wish lists. Included in the photograph collection are lists of buildings he wanted to photograph. Today, the list is crucial to a history of jazz because so many of those sites are gone.

Russell's relationship with Manuel "Fess" Manetta was special because "the professor" was one of his mentors. As Russell went about New Orleans photographing early jazz sites, he would carefully note on the back of the photograph whether he had checked out his information with Manetta. He recorded hundreds of hours of interviews with Fess. Manetta recounted his early days in Storyville, enlivening the hours of oral history with renditions of favored compositions on his out-of-tune piano. Russell's deep-seated integrity and feeling of responsibility toward the musicians he worked with is shown in the written agreement he made with Manetta. If he should ever publish a book about Fess (once revenues had covered the costs of photography and typing), any profits would be shared equally between Russell and Manetta.

Determined as he was to save everything, Russell also acquired Manetta's books, sheet music collection, musical instruments, and music instruction books. The Manetta papers give a real sense of a professional jazz teacher's world, as well as the development of Algiers, where Manetta lived, in the early decades of the twentieth century.

Russell also maintained what he referred to as his jazz files — an eclectic mix of items. Included are miscellaneous letters and an enormous amount of ephemera, such as announcements for Lil (Mrs. Louis) Armstrong's diner featuring "Rug Cutter's Roast" and "Dipsy Doodle Noodles."

Proud of his record collection, Russell noted that certain recordings had once belonged to Louis Armstrong. While he maintained his paper documents carefully wrapped in plastic bags from the corner A&P, his record collection was housed in wooden record-shipping crates. Frustrated with commercially available record players, he built his own machine, capable of playing records accurately at different speeds. His record collection is invaluable — both for the quality and scarcity of the recordings and for their carefully preserved original jackets, themselves collectors' items.

All his collections were maintained in specific order. The sheet music collection was arranged in the following sequence: pieces

Bill Russell with record boxes, probably at his record shop

Clarinetists Jimmy Granato and Barney Bigard with Natty Dominique and Bill
Russell backstage at the Chicago Theatre, February 1954. Photograph by Billy Ky

printed in New Orleans, the extremely rare, and musical style. His postcard collection was organized by locale and his books, by topic. His role as a consultant to jazz musicians on copyright issues is clearly evident in the large number of volumes relating to copyright law. His pamphlet collection demonstrates his view that jazz arose in the context of the musical culture of New Orleans. In it are pamphlets about the French Opera House and the 1894 German North American Singing Festival held in a specially constructed theater at Lee Circle, information on train service in New Orleans (since musicians usually traveled by train), and telephone books, which Russell used to locate musicians' addresses. Other items, such as the keys from Storyville entrepreneur Tom Anderson's piano and part of the railing in Economy Hall, defy the imagination.

His periodical collection epitomizes his quest for information. He gathered rare numbers from throughout the United States and the world. Most items in this collection are so unusual that only about a third of them appear in standard library bibliographic tools.

Bill Russell's collection is a reflection of his reputation and knowledge as a jazz historian. He could not turn away anyone seeking information or wanting to talk about New Orleans music. Just as jazz musicians trusted Russell, the Historic New Orleans Collection is proud to be entrusted with caring for his legacy. By making his collection available to the public, we hope to continue his spirit of generosity.

—Alfred E. Lemmon

"A Bad Night," according to Russell's note. Bill Russell and Alfred Lion recording at San Jacinto Hall, well-known jazz site on Dumaine Street, August 1944

SOURCES

Jazz Scrapbook explores William Russell's relationships with the pioneering musicians he admired. The primary source for each essay is the William Russell Jazz Collection. The collection is available to all researchers at the Historic New Orleans Collection's Williams Research Center, 410 Chartres Street, New Orleans.

Chilton, John. *Who's Who of Jazz.* Philadelphia, 1972.

Fairweather, Digby. *Jazz: The Rough Guide.* London, 1995.

Gara, Larry. *The Baby Dodds Story.* Baton Rouge, 1992.

Gushee, Lawrence. "A Preliminary Chronology of the Early Career of Ferd 'Jelly Roll' Morton." *American Music* 3 (Winter 1985): 389-412.

_____. "When Was Bunk Johnson Born and Why Should We Care?" *The Jazz Archivist* 2(November 1987): 4-6.

Hazeldine, Mike, ed. and comp. *Bill Russell's American Music.* New Orleans, 1993.

Hentoff, Nat. "Max Roach: The Unsubservient Drummer." *The Progressive* (May 1981): 52-53.

Jones, Max, and John Chilton. *Louis: The Louis Armstrong Story, 1900-1971.* New York, 1971.

Ramsey, Frederic, Jr., and Charles Edward Smith, eds. *Jazzmen.* New York, 1939.

Rose, Al. *Storyville.* Tuscaloosa, 1974.

Russell, Bill. Interview by William R. Hogan, 4 September 1962. William Ransom Hogan Jazz Archive, Tulane University.

Russell, Bill. *New Orleans Style.* Edited and compiled by Barry Martyn and Mike Hazeldine. New Orleans, 1994.

CONTRIBUTORS

Carol O. Bartels, documentation coordinator at the Historic New Orleans Collection, received a B.A. in social science education and an M.A. in history with a concentration in archives and records administration from the University of New Orleans.

Patricia Brady is director of publications at the Historic New Orleans Collection and coeditor of *Jazz Scrapbook*. She is a cultural and social historian with a Ph.D. from Tulane University.

Mark Cave holds a B.A. in history from Ohio University and an M.L.I.S. degree from the University of Kentucky. He serves as reference archivist at the Collection's Williams Research Center, where the William Russell Jazz Collection is made available to researchers.

Louise Hoffman, coeditor of *Jazz Scrapbook,* edits the *Historic New Orleans Collection Quarterly.* She is a graduate of the University of North Carolina at Chapel Hill.

Richard Jackson served for twenty-five years as head of the Americana Collection in the New York Public Library's music division at Lincoln Center until his retirement. He is a volunteer at the Williams Research Center.

Jon Kukla is director of the Historic New Orleans Collection, an authority on early southern political and intellectual history, and a lapsed saxophone player. He earned his Ph.D. at the University of Toronto and enjoys writing about a wide range of subjects.

M. Theresa LeFevre studied archives and records management after a teaching career in the Orleans Parish schools. She is registrar of manuscripts at the Collection.

Alfred E. Lemmon, curator of manuscripts at the Williams Research Center, received a Ph.D. in Latin American Studies from Tulane University. An authority on the music of the Americas, he has overseen the processing of the William Russell Jazz Collection since its acquisition in 1992.

John Magill is curator in charge of the reading room at the Williams Research Center. He holds an M.A. in history from the University of New Orleans and has written and lectured extensively about the urban development of New Orleans.

Dan B. Ross spent many years in the Southwest before returning to New Orleans to pursue an interest in New Orleans music. He is currently helping to process the William Russell Jazz Collection.

Nancy Ruck, a graduate of Sarah Lawrence College, has worked at the Museum of Broadcasting in New York City and at Rockefeller University. She is manuscripts cataloguer at the Historic New Orleans Collection where she is cataloguing the William Russell Jazz Collection.

THE HISTORIC
NEW ORLEANS COLLECTION

Founded in 1966, the Historic New Orleans Collection is supported by the Kemper and Leila Williams Foundation. The institutional mission embraces acquiring and preserving books, manuscripts, and visual materials that document the history and culture of New Orleans and Louisiana; promoting the study and appreciation of this history and its context through the Williams Research Center, museum exhibitions, publications, and other programs; and maintaining a complex of historic French Quarter buildings including the Williams Residence house museum.

ABOUT THE BOOK

Jazz Scrapbook is an informal collection of essays and candid photographs reflecting Bill Russell's devotion to New Orleans jazz — its origins, history, and musicians. It is a sampling of the vast amount of information in the William Russell Jazz Collection but is by no means a comprehensive study.

The essayists of this volume know the collection intimately, indeed almost know Bill Russell through his collection, and have presented an inside view of Russell and his relationships with important jazz musicians. Since the acquisition of the collection nearly six years ago, the Historic New Orleans Collection's curator of manuscripts, Alfred E. Lemmon, has coordinated all aspects of processing, dealing with the problems presented by recorded material and making the collection available to eager music historians and other researchers. Bruce Boyd Raeburn, director of the Hogan Jazz Archive, has been a valuable consultant, reading and commenting on this manuscript. Nancy Ruck has been responsible for cataloguing manuscripts and other materials from the beginning, with the able volunteer assistance of Richard Jackson and Dan B. Ross. Other essayists — manuscripts and reading room professionals at the Collection's Williams Research Center — have been mainstays of the cooperative effort necessary to process such a large collection.

Seated, left to right, Nancy Ruck, Richard Jackson, Carol Bartels, Alfred Lemmon, Patricia Brady, Dan Ross, Mark Cave; standing, Michael Ledet, Theresa LeFevre, Jon Kukla, John Magill, and Louise Hoffman in the Williams Research Center, repository of the William Russell Jazz Collection. Photograph by Jan White Brantley

KEMPER AND LEILA WILLIAMS FOUNDATION

THE HISTORIC NEW ORLEANS COLLECTION

Board of Directors

Mrs. William K. Christovich, President
G. Henry Pierson, Jr.
John E. Walker
Fred M. Smith
Suzanne T. Mestayer

Dr. Jon Kukla, Director

Dr. Patricia Brady, Director of Publications
Louise C. Hoffman, Editor

Body copy: Avenir; headlines: Bureau Agency
Paper: 70 lb. Lakewood text

Book design and production
Michael Ledet art & design, New Orleans, Louisiana

Typography
Billie M. Cox, Jr., New Orleans, Louisiana

Printing
BookCrafters, Chelsea, Michigan

Bunk Johnson at the Stuyvesant Casino, New York City, 1945